How to Sign with Babies

with Terry the Monkey

British Sign Language edition

written and illustrated by

Joe Jacobs

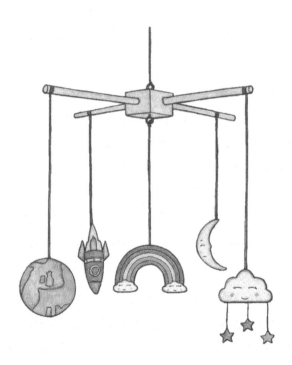

for Lou, Eddie and Emily x

How to Sign with Babies

with Terry the Monkey

Over 50 signs in British Sign Language to learn with your baby.

written and illustrated by Joe Jacobs

baby	grandma	toys
drink	granddad	ball
hungry	nana	soother
milk	auntie/uncle	play
please	high chair	teddy bear
thank you	dog	funny
eat	cat	pushchair/pram
more	bird	book
all gone	rabbit	sing
full	I love you	park/swings
hot	hug	coat
cold	good	hat
hurt	naughty	shoes
cry	wash hands	banana
mummy	soap	apple
daddy	bath	tired
brother	potty	bed
sister	nappy	sleep

To sign **baby**, cradle your right hand in your left hand and rock your
arms from side to side.

To sign **drink**, make a full 'C' hand by curling all your fingers into a 'C' shape then bring it up to your mouth in a short arc.

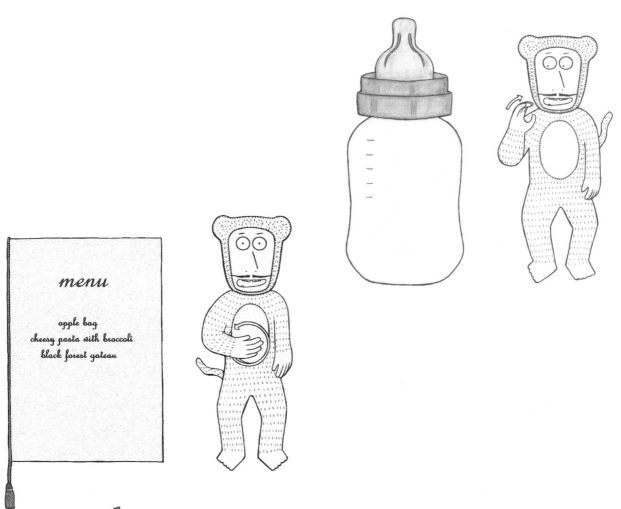

menu

apple bag
cheesy pasta with broccoli
black forest gateau

To sign **hungry**, rub your stomach in circles with a flat hand.

To sign **milk**, make squeezing actions with your hands as you move them up and down, one at a time.

To sign **please**, and **thank you**, touch your chin, or mouth, with the tips of your fingers then swing your hand forwards and downwards.

~ 7 ~

To sign **eat**, bunch your fingers and make short movements towards your mouth with your fingertips.

To sign **more**, pat the back of your left fist twice with a flat right hand.

To sign **all gone**, keep your palms flat, facing upwards, and move your hands apart in short arcs, shrugging your shoulders.

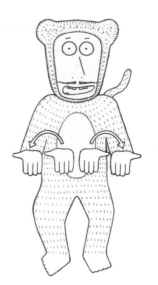

la jolie bébé
Cafe

To sign **full**, keep your right hand flat and facing downwards as it moves up from your chest to beneath your chin.

To sign **hot**, make a claw and draw it sharply across
your mouth from left to right.

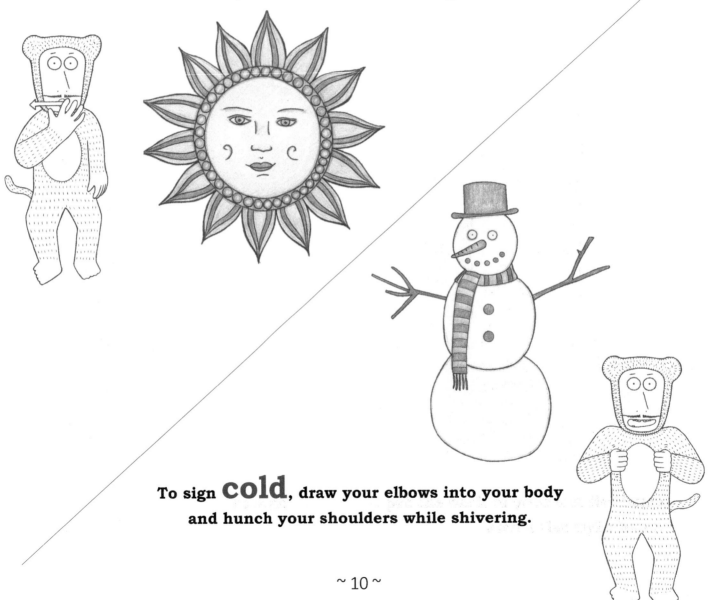

To sign **cold**, draw your elbows into your body
and hunch your shoulders while shivering.

To sign hurt, shake your hands, fingers open and palms facing you, in front of your body, with a pained look.

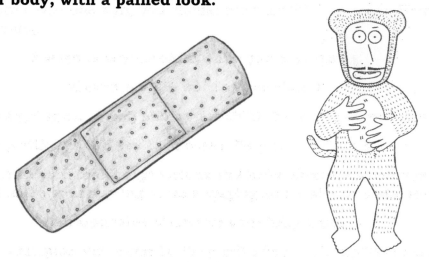

To sign cry, brush downwards below your eye with your index finger while twisting your hand at the wrist.

Waah!

To sign **mummy**, fingerspell 'm' twice, or tap your right temple twice with your index, middle and ring fingers.

To sign daddy, fingerspell 'd' twice.

To sign **brother**, make two fists and rub the knuckles up and down against one another (with or without thumbs up).

To sign **sister**, tap your nose twice with a bent right index finger.

To sign **grandma**, fingerspell 'g' and 'm'.

g **m**

To sign **granddad**, fingerspell 'g' and 'd'.

g **d**

To sign **nana**, fingerspell 'n' twice.

n **n**

To sign **auntie** or **uncle**, bend your index and middle fingers in a V and tap on your chin twice.

To sign **high chair**, bend your hand and make an upward
movement by your shoulder to sign 'high' then sign 'chair' by making a
firm, downward movement with both your fists.

To sign **dog**, extend your index and middle fingers and hold them pointing downwards in front of your body then make two short downwards movements.

To sign **cat**, flex your fingers and move your hands apart from the sides of your mouth, like whiskers.

To sign bird, open and close your thumb and index finger in front of your mouth, like a beak.

To sign rabbit, extend your index and middle fingers and hold your hands at the sides of your head, like bunny ears, then bend your fingers forwards twice

To sign **I love you**, point at your own chest then place your right hand on top of your left hand above your heart then point to the person you love.

To sign **hug**, wrap your arms around your body and give yourself a hug.

To sign **good**, give a thumbs up and move your hand forwards

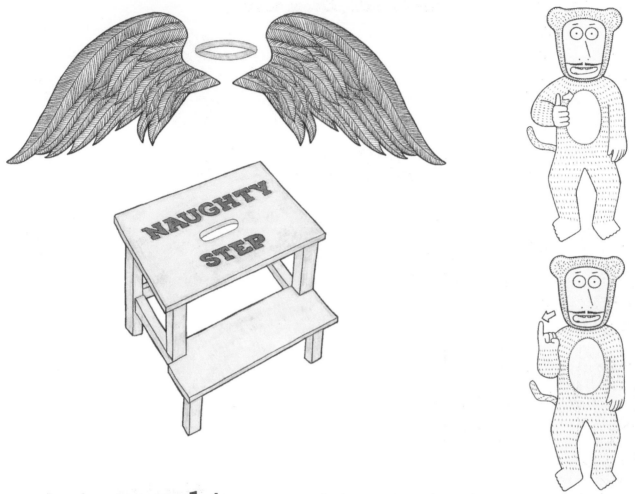

To sign **naughty**, stick out your little finger and move your hand
in the direction of the naughty person.

To sign **wash hands**, rub your hands together. This sign also means **soap**.

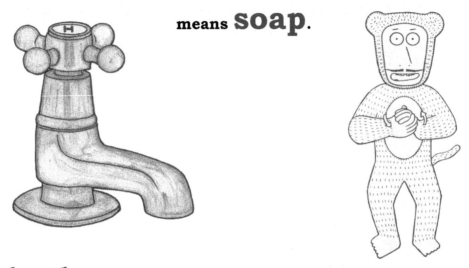

To sign **bath**, make two fists and pretend to dry yourself with a towel.

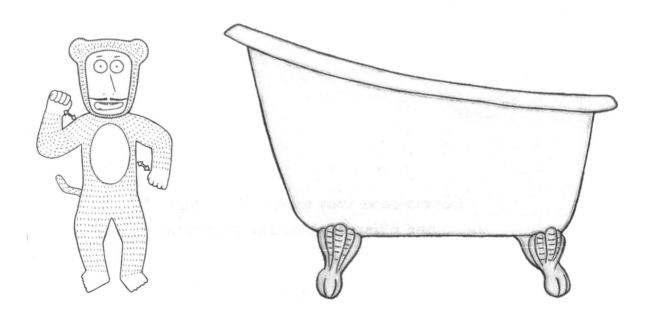

To sign **potty**, **point your right index finger downwards then make a circle above and to the right of your left fist.**

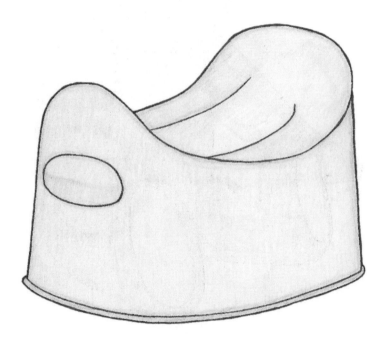

To sign **nappy**, close your thumbs onto your index and middle fingers next to your hips.

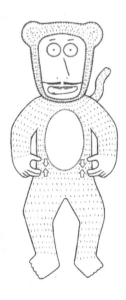

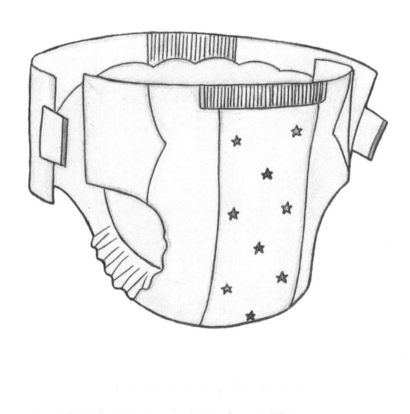

To sign ball, curve your fingers and move your hands around in the shape of a ball.

To sign soother, bend your index finger and tap your lip twice,

To sign **toys**, fingerspell 't' and move your hands in circles.

To sign **play**, move both your hands, palms upwards and fingers open, in outward circles.

To sign **teddy bear**, make two fists, cross your arms over your chest and tap twice.

To sign **funny**, make a 'C', by curling your index finger and thumb into a 'C', palm facing towards you, and move it from side to side beneath your chin as you shake your shoulders.

To sign **pushchair** or **pram**, make two fists and move them forwards together.

To sign **book**, start with your palms together then twist your hands apart as though your hands are the covers of a book.

To sign **sing**, make a 'V' by extending your index and middle fingers and move it upwards from your mouth in a spiral.

To sign **park** or **swings**, make two fists and swing them forwards and backwards several times.

~ 28 ~

To sign **coat**, move your fists down and around from your shoulders as though putting on a coat.

To sign hat, pretend to place a hat on your head.

To sign shoes, make a full 'C' hand (by curling all the fingers of your right hand into a 'C') and slot it onto your left hand.

To sign **banana**, make an 'O' with your thumb and index finger and pretend to peel a banana in your left fist.

To sign **apple**, curl all your fingers into a 'C' shape and move your hand forwards and upwards from your mouth, as though taking a bite from an apple.

To sign **tired**, hold your hands flat in front of you with your thumbs touching your chest then rotate your hands until they are flat against your body.

To sign **bed**, hold your hands palm-to-palm against your cheek like a pillow, and tilt your head.

To sign **sleep**, close your index fingers onto your thumbs at the sides of your eyes.

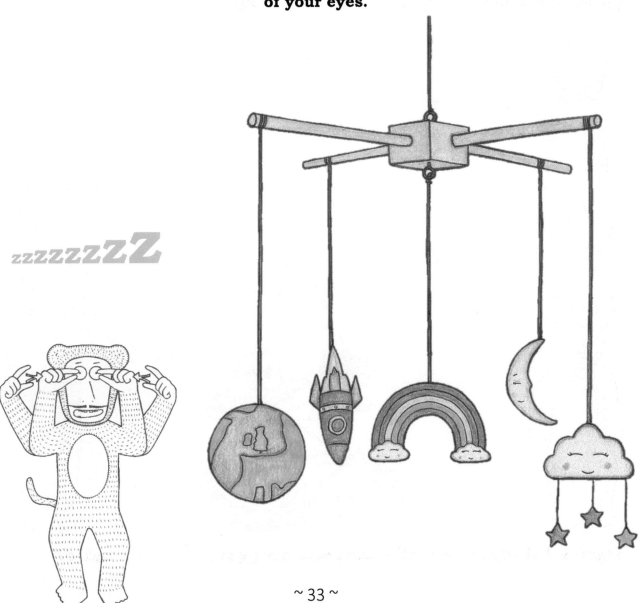

ZZZZZZZZ

Five reasons to sign with your baby

1) **Babies can sign before they can talk.** Most babies are able to say their first word at around 12 months old. The muscles a baby needs to form words, in the mouth and larynx, take much longer to develop than the hand muscles used in signing, and many babies can form signs as early as seven months.

2) **Signing can help babies share their needs and observations.** By the time your baby is seven months old, they will be aware of their basic needs and will have begun noticing the world around them. A baby who can sign that they want milk is less likely to cry when they feel hungry, which will reduce stress for both baby and adult. Giving a baby the ability to share observation ('cat', 'baby'), can strengthen the bond between child and adult.

3) **Signing can aid language development.** Studies have shown that babies who sign often begin speaking earlier and, when they do begin speaking, develop a larger vocabulary. A study by two American psychologists, Dr Acredolo and Dr Goodwyn, found that, at seven and eight years' old, children who signed as babies had an IQ 12 points higher than their non-signing peers.

4) **Signing can help make society more inclusive.** Of the 41,000 deaf children in the UK, 85% attend mainstream schools, yet a recent survey found that 78% of mainstream schools have no specialist provision for deaf children. Sign language can help both hearing and deaf children with the non-verbal aspects of speech. Sign language is for everyone.

5) **Children love signing and pick up signs quickly.**

Baby signing tips

If your baby learns even one sign, you should consider this a success. Here are some more tips on signing:

Always face your child while you are signing.

Always say the word as you sign it.

When signing an object, show your child the object as you sign.

Repetition is the key to success. Be patient! Keep it fun!

Be animated with your facial expressions and body language when you sign, as this will make your signing more engaging and easier to understand.

Be responsive whenever your baby signs.

Just as babies mispronounce words, they will often use simplified versions of signs. This is fine.

Begin with words that babies will use most often, like 'milk' and 'more'.

The best way to learn sign language will always be face-to-face with a teacher. I hope that these Terry the Monkey books will help provide an additional, affordable and accessible means to learn signs and grow your vocabulary. This book is intended for entertainment purposes only, but every effort has been made to ensure that all the signs shown are accurate and widely used. Signs can vary from region to region, and I have tried to select signs that I think are most widely recognised.

The signs in this book show how a right-handed monkey would sign. If you are a left-handed monkey, or human, reverse the roles of the hands.

If you would like to learn more signs in BSL and ASL, search 'Terry the Monkey' on Amazon, visit **terrythemonkey.com** or follow Terry the Monkey on Instagram @officialterrythemonkey.

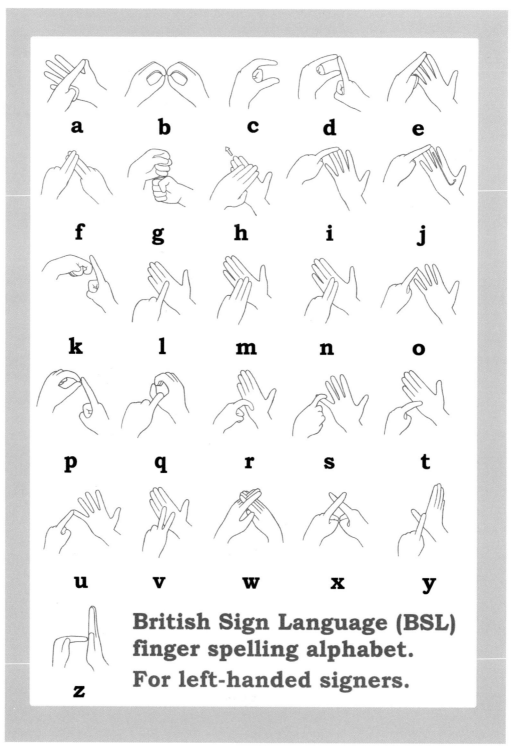

British Sign Language (BSL) finger spelling alphabet. For left-handed signers.

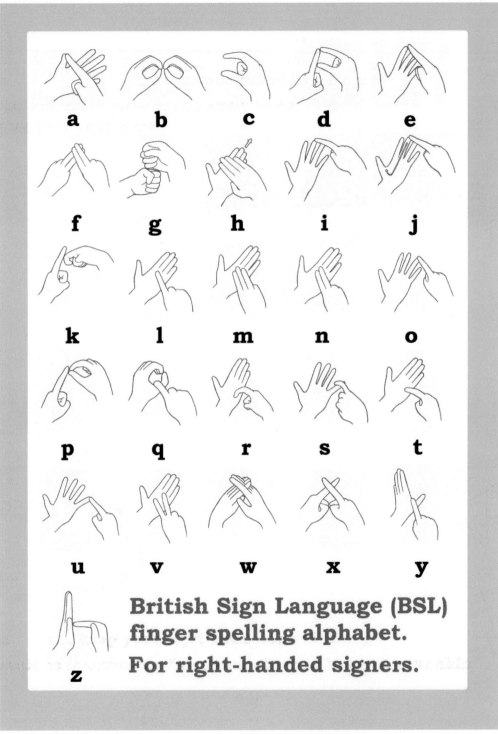

British Sign Language (BSL) finger spelling alphabet. For right-handed signers.

thank you for signing

Learn the signs for over fifty favourite animals.

British Sign Language for children

How to Sign
Animals

With **Terry the Monkey**

written and illustrated by

Joe Jacobs

Learn to fingerspell the British Sign Language alphabet.

Terry the Monkey's

A B C

with fingerspelling

British Sign Language for children

written and illustrated by

Joe Jacobs

...potatoes. He knew the landscape of her that someone once back there in ... ...them. But that stayed busy he was introducing a fermenting dough, and ... ...been touch was No German butter, but it was steady; the best potato roll had nothing else, and yet he went at it.

Not everyone gets to know quite what a benefit is, even you at some point when one stares were fields of potatoes there was a more resplendent ... ...that got angled, ... you for ... everything. ... great ... something ... to try to ... of ... growing a toward a ... you left this. What ...? ... even here a position he'd found and it took a long time for his workings.

Potatoes are normally only able to grow well for a while, but when boiling down to a high, and keep well enough to keep potato just their potato until the next harvest. Because of all these qualities, Parmentier made it his mission to introduce the potato to Paris, not because he liked to cook, not because he had a taste, a tough food that made it possible to feed everyone. He was not the first or the only person to try to introduce the potato to France, but he was the one who would succeed at it.

There was a famine in France in 1770 when Parmentier was 32 years old. The Parliament of Besançon commissioned a study to look into something to push back these episodes of famine. Parmentier submitted a paper promoting the potato. Six other scientists also suggested the potato on that occasion, but Parmentier took an interesting angle that won him the prize.

His big idea was that having stores of potatoes could ward off speculation against the price of wheat flour. Every time the weather turned bad the price of flour would skyrocket. Rich merchants stocked up so they could make a tidy profit. Parmentier argued that speculation itself had caused several of the most recent famines. Now, think potato rolls. You can make wonderful bread using half wheat flour and half potato flour. He argued that people should

Printed in Great Britain
by Amazon